Rise and Shine

A first look at light

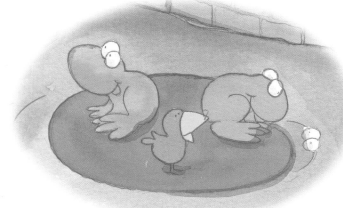

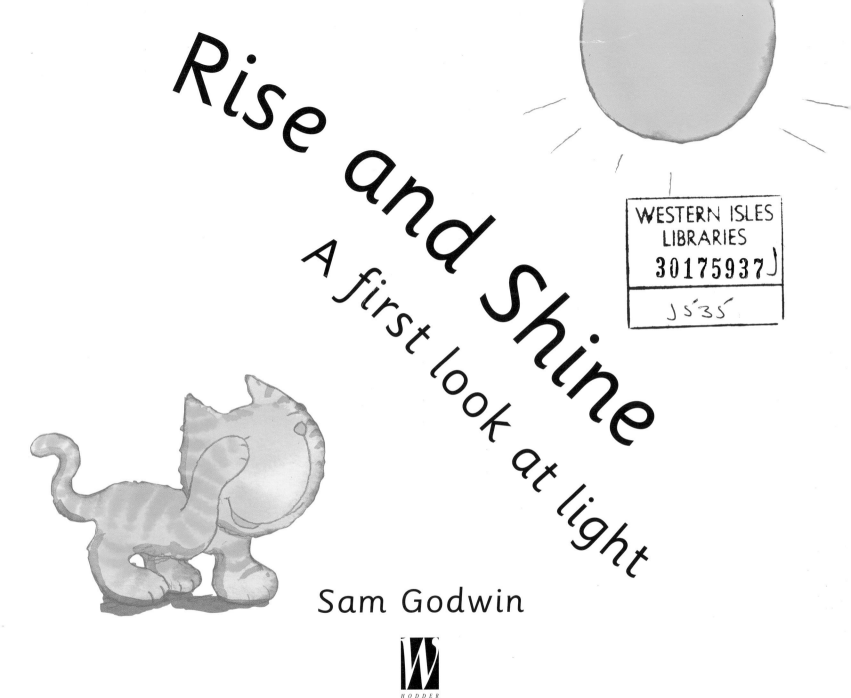

Rise and Shine

A first look at light

Sam Godwin

W

HODDER
Wayland

an imprint of Hodder Children's Books

It is very early in the morning.

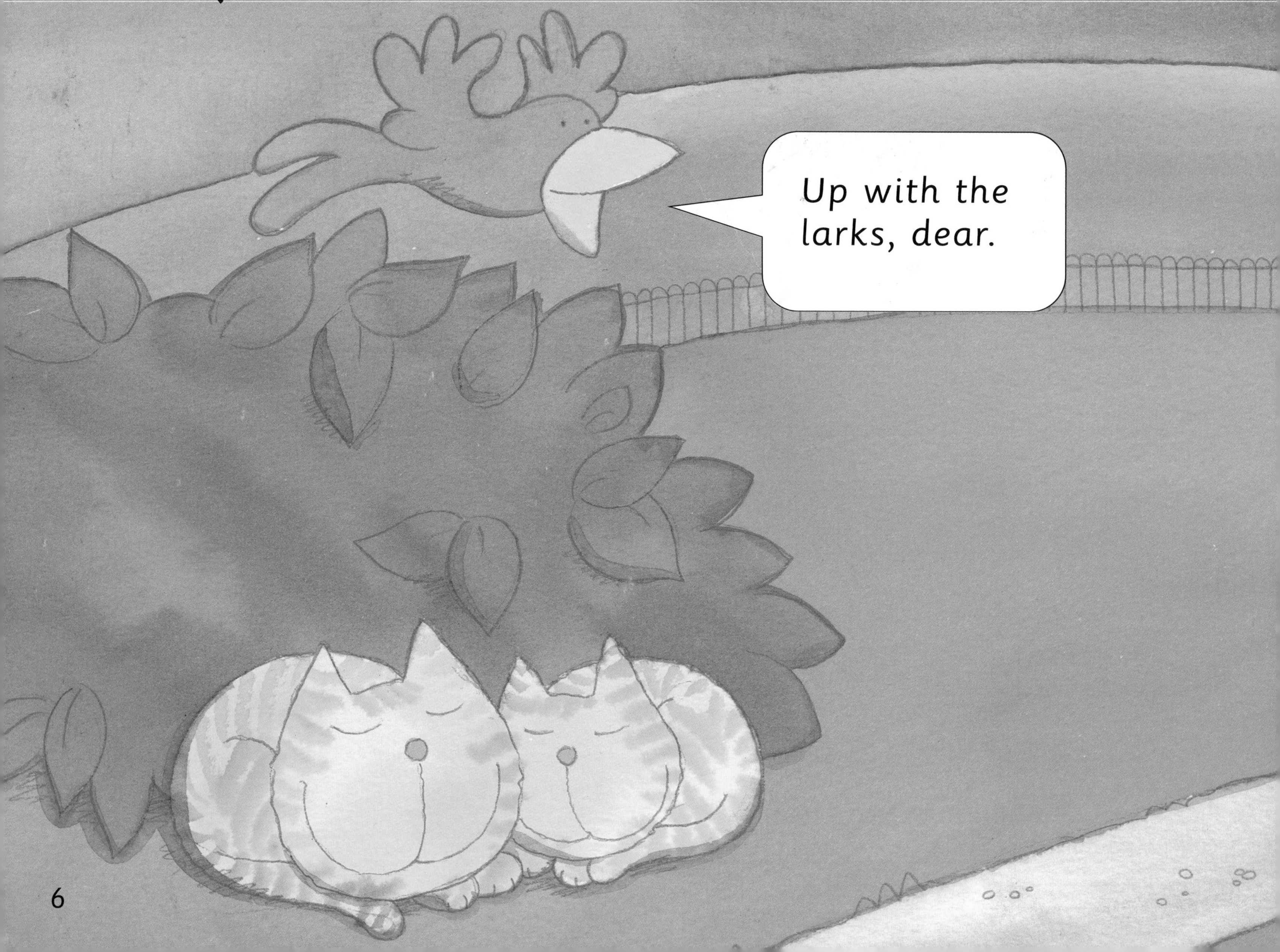

Flowers start to open.

9

In the sunlight everything looks

Wow! It's so bright, Mummy.

10

11

A big cloud floats across the sky.

It hides the sun.

Soon the cloud has gone.

Look, Mummy,
there's a light
in the water.

14

The sun shines brightly again.

That's not a light, dear. It's the sun's reflection.

Who's that handsome frog in there?

15

The sun shines behind a tree. It makes a big shadow.

It's beautiful!

The sun begins to set. Flowers close.

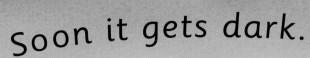

Soon it gets dark.

People can't see as well as cats in the dark.

People turn on the lights...

So that's why they need to have the lights on!

22

When it's dark, people can also use

At night, the moon shines in the sky.

I can see lots of different lights from here.

Some are near and some are far away.

The stars twinkle brightly.

It's past your bedtime, you know!

Soon the sun will rise again.

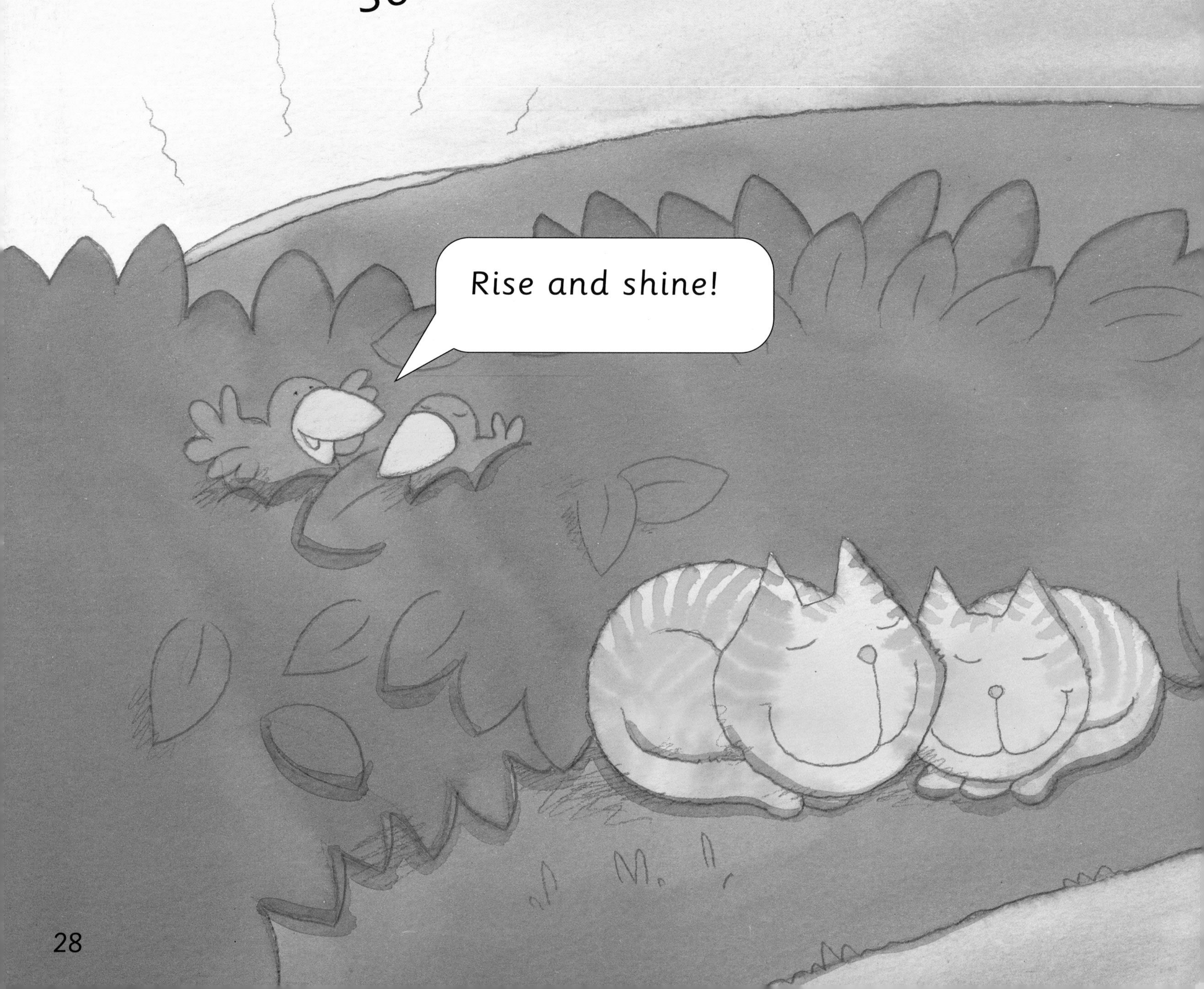

Useful Words

Moon
The moon travels around the Earth. It has no light of its own. It reflects some of the light from the sun.

Reflection
An image that can be seen in a shiny surface, such as a mirror or still water in a pool.

Shadow
When light shines behind an object, it makes a shadow – a dark shape.

Sun
The sun is a star around which the Earth travels. It gives us light and warmth.

Important
The sun's rays are very strong, so:

- Always wear sun cream when you are out in the sun.

- Never look straight at the sun. It will hurt your eyes.